Minerals as Necessary Nutrients

BY C. M. DAVIS

Kids Core

An Imprint of Abdo Publishing
abdobooks.com

abdobooks.com

Published by Abdo Publishing, a division of ABDO, PO Box 398166, Minneapolis, Minnesota 55439. Copyright © 2023 by Abdo Consulting Group, Inc. International copyrights reserved in all countries. No part of this book may be reproduced in any form without written permission from the publisher. Kids Core™ is a trademark and logo of Abdo Publishing.

Printed in the United States of America, North Mankato, Minnesota.
102022
012023

THIS BOOK CONTAINS RECYCLED MATERIALS

Cover Photo: Shutterstock Images
Interior Photos: Prostock Studio/Shutterstock Images, 4–5, 14; Tatjana Baibakova/Shutterstock Images, 6; iStockphoto, 8; Monkey Business Images/Shutterstock Images, 10–11, 26; Shutterstock Images, 12, 16–17, 24, 28 (top), 29 (top); Juefra Photo/iStockphoto, 18; Antonov Maxim/Shutterstock Images, 20; People Images/iStockphoto, 22; Marian Weyo/Shutterstock Images, 28 (bottom); Looker Studio/Shutterstock Images, 29 (bottom)

Editor: Ann Schwab
Series Designer: Layna Darling

Library of Congress Control Number: 2022940677

Publisher's Cataloging-in-Publication Data

Names: Davis, C. M., author.
Title: Minerals as necessary nutrients / by C. M. Davis
Description: Minneapolis, Minnesota: Abdo Publishing, 2023 | Series: Necessary nutrients | Includes online resources and index.
Identifiers: ISBN 9781098290030 (lib. bdg.) | ISBN 9781098275235 (ebook)
Subjects: LCSH: Minerals--Juvenile literature. | Minerals in the body--Juvenile literature. | Minerals in human nutrition--Juvenile literature. | Nutrition--Health aspects--Juvenile literature.
Classification: DDC 613.2--dc23

CONTENTS

CHAPTER 1
A Vital Nutrient 4

CHAPTER 2
How Bodies Use Minerals 10

CHAPTER 3
Minerals in Food 16

Nutrient Jobs 28
Glossary 30
Online Resources 31
Learn More 31
Index 32
About the Author 32

Food items used in baking often contain minerals and other nutrients.

A Vital Nutrient

It's baking day! On Saturdays Ayana and her mom always bake a yummy treat. Today they are making raisin bread. They set out flour, raisins, oil, and other items on the kitchen table. First, they mix yeast, warm water, and sugar together in a big bowl.

The mineral iodine is found in many foods, such as fish, potatoes, eggs, and cranberries.

After five minutes, it begins to bubble and foam. This means it is time to add salt. Ayana picks up the salt container. She reads a new word on the label.

"Mom, what does *iodized* mean?" she asks.

"A mineral called iodine has been added to this salt," her mom replies. "Most people use salt when they cook food. Adding iodine to salt helps make sure people get enough of this mineral."

Ayana pours a teaspoon of salt into the bowl. Then she asks, "Is iodine in other foods too?"

"Yes. After we put our bread in the oven, let's get your tablet. We can do some research."

"Yay!" Ayana says, smiling.

Iodine

Iodine is found in seawater and in soil near the ocean. It helps the **thyroid** work well. It also helps the brain grow. Iodine is found in seafood, milk, eggs, and other foods.

The meat and milk of plant-eating animals contain minerals.

What Are Minerals?

Minerals are natural substances found in rocks and water. The human body uses minerals to grow and develop. The body needs 16 different minerals to stay healthy.

The body cannot make minerals. People must get them from food. People get minerals by eating plants. Minerals can also come from eating the eggs, milk, and meat of animals. Minerals help the body in many ways.

Further Evidence

Look at the website below. Does it give any new evidence to support Chapter One?

Mineral

abdocorelibrary.com/minerals-as-necessary-nutrients

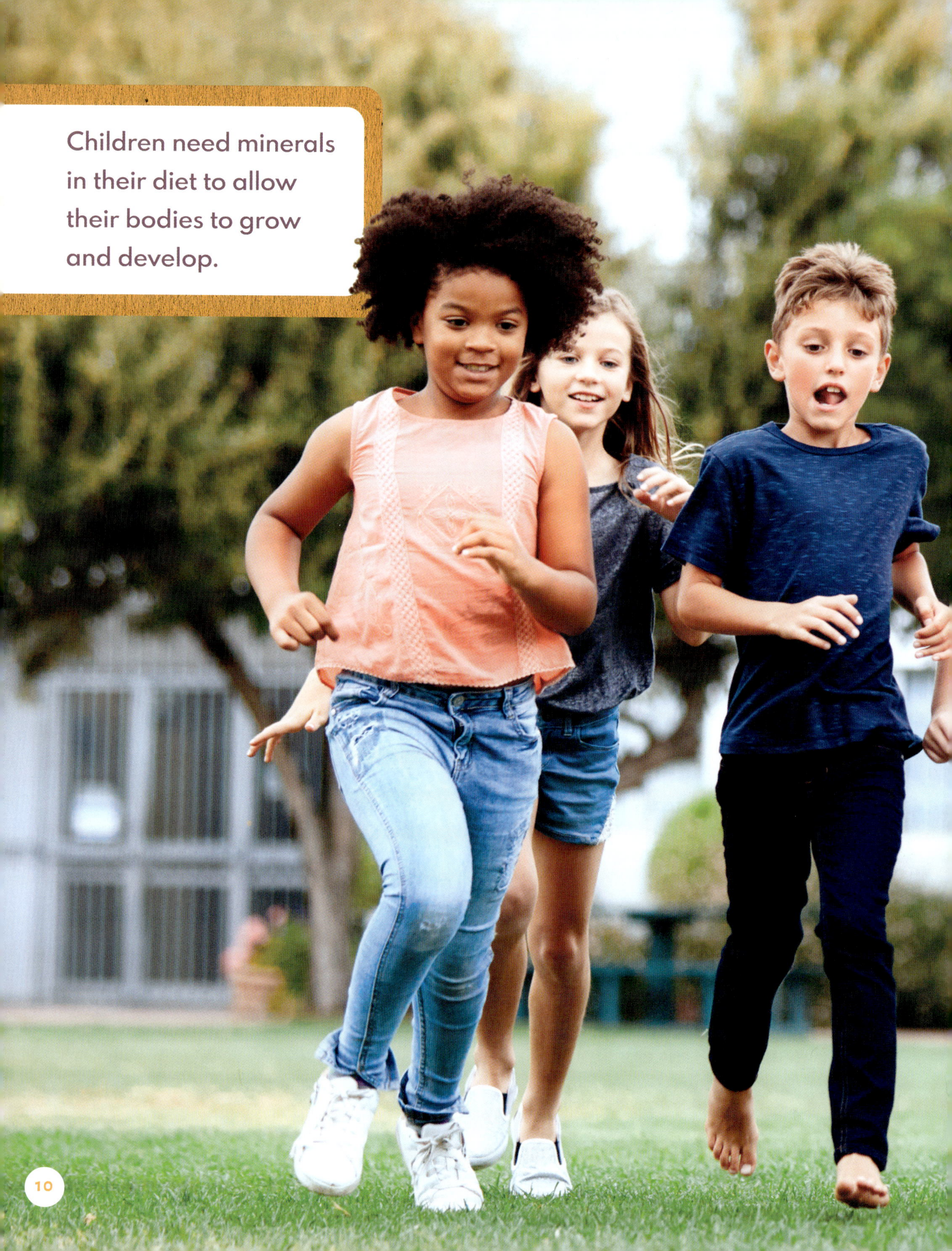

Children need minerals in their diet to allow their bodies to grow and develop.

CHAPTER 2

How Bodies Use Minerals

Minerals are **micronutrients**. All living beings need them to grow and stay well. There are two groups of minerals that the body needs. These are called major minerals and **trace minerals**.

Most toothpastes contain fluoride. This mineral strengthens teeth and helps prevent cavities.

The body needs larger amounts of major minerals. These are calcium, chloride, magnesium, phosphorus, potassium, sodium, and sulfur.

The body needs only a little bit of trace minerals. Examples include cobalt, copper, fluoride, iron, iodine, manganese, molybdenum, selenium, and zinc.

Minerals at Work

Minerals help the human body with many tasks. Calcium helps build strong bones and teeth. Fluoride works to prevent tooth decay.

Plant Food

Healthy soil contains a lot of minerals, including calcium and iron. Plants grown in rich soil will soak up minerals through their roots. When people and animals eat these plants, they get more minerals. This can help them stay healthy.

Sulfur helps keep hair strong.

Sodium maintains the proper balance of water inside and outside of the body's cells.

Manganese helps turn food into energy. Sulfur keeps hair, skin, and nails healthy. Zinc aids in repairing the taste buds on the tongue so people can taste food.

Minerals also work to keep the **immune system** healthy. This system stops germs from entering the body. It also helps people recover from illness and injury.

Nutrition expert Jennifer Willoughby teaches children how to make healthy food choices. She recommends snack foods such as berries and nuts that have lots of **nutrients**:

> They have fiber, they have protein, they have vitamins and minerals, [and] they have iron and a lot of things children need for development.

Source: "5 Foods That Pack a Nutritional Punch." *Call & Post*, 23 Sept. 2015, p. 3B, proquest.com. Accessed 4 May 2022.

What's the Big Idea?

Read the quote carefully. What is the main idea? Explain how the main idea is supported by details.

The nutrients people eat provide them with energy and keep their bodies healthy.

CHAPTER 3

Minerals in Food

Food is made up of many different nutrients. Carbohydrates, fats, protein, fiber, vitamins, and minerals are nutrients. After people eat, their bodies break the food down into these nutrients. Then their blood carries the nutrients all around their bodies.

Healthy meals include a variety of food types.

The body needs only small amounts of minerals. People need different amounts of minerals at different ages. Children need smaller amounts of minerals than adults do.

People usually get the minerals they need through their meals. Calcium is found in milk and other dairy products. Grapes and other fruits are good sources of fluoride. It is often added to toothpaste too. Sulfur is present in turkey, beef, nuts, and other protein foods. Zinc is found in many foods, such as beef and yogurt. It is important that people eat a wide variety of foods so the body gets enough minerals. They need to eat from each food group every day.

Eating for Good Health

Magnesium

Iodine

Phosphorus

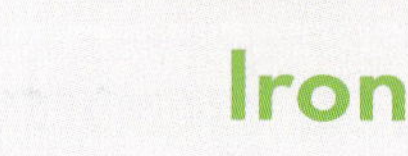

Iron

Potassium

Calcium

People can receive the important minerals they need by eating a healthy diet. These nutrients are found in a wide variety of foods.

What Are the Food Groups?

There are five different food groups. These are fruits, vegetables, grains, protein foods, and dairy. Each meal should include foods from more than one food group.

Children up to ten years old need two to three servings of fruits each day. This includes foods such as apples, oranges, and grapes. They also need two to three servings of vegetables. Some good choices are tomatoes, carrots, and sweet potatoes. Broccoli, Brussels sprouts, and spinach are also rich in minerals.

Stir-frying is a cooking method that helps keep nutrients in food.

Children should also eat five to six servings of grains. Cereal, bread, and pasta are foods made from grains. At least half of these servings should be from whole grains. Brown rice, oatmeal, and whole wheat bread are examples of whole grains. Having two or three servings of protein every day is also important for children. Eggs, beans, meat, fish, and tofu provide protein. Children should eat two to three servings of dairy foods every day. Good dairy choices are milk, cheese, and yogurt.

Save the Minerals!

Boiling foods often causes minerals to be lost in cooking water. Steaming and stir-frying help keep more minerals in foods. Microwaving food with a small amount of water is another good cooking method.

Minerals such as calcium, iron, and zinc are often added to breakfast cereal.

These serving suggestions are all general guidelines. People should talk to their doctors to learn the best amounts for them. Minerals can also be added to foods. This gives the food more nutrients. Some foods that often have added minerals are salt, breakfast cereal, and whole wheat bread.

A Healthy Balance

Not getting enough of a mineral can make a person sick. An example is not getting enough calcium. This may cause teeth and bones to become weak. Getting too much of a mineral can also make a person sick. This can happen if a person eats too much sodium. That can raise blood pressure too high. It could harm the heart and other organs.

Taking extra minerals is usually not necessary if people eat a well-balanced diet. Sometimes a doctor might recommend taking **supplements**.

Well-balanced meals normally supply people with all the minerals they need to stay healthy.

An example is when a person has an allergy to milk. This may make it hard for the person to get enough calcium.

Minerals are needed for people to live and grow. Their bodies cannot function without them. Eating a proper diet provides people with the minerals they need. It keeps the entire body healthy and working well.

Explore Online

Visit the website below. What new information does it provide that wasn't mentioned in Chapter Three?

Why Can't I Eat Cupcakes for Dinner?

abdocorelibrary.com/minerals-as-necessary-nutrients

Nutrient Jobs

Calcium helps build strong bones and teeth.

Fluoride works to prevent tooth decay.

Zinc helps repair
taste buds.

Sulfur keeps hair, skin,
and nails healthy.

Glossary

immune system
a network of cells, proteins, and organs in the body that fight disease

iodized
had iodine added

micronutrients
vitamins and minerals needed by the body

nutrients
substances needed for the body's health

supplements
pills, gummies, or liquids that provide minerals and other nutrients

thyroid
a gland in the body that helps control many body functions, such as temperature, blood pressure, and heart rate

trace minerals
minerals that the body needs in very small amounts

Online Resources

To learn more about minerals as necessary nutrients, visit our free resource websites below.

Visit **abdocorelibrary.com** or scan this QR code for free Common Core resources for teachers and students, including vetted activities, multimedia, and booklinks, for deeper subject comprehension.

Visit **abdobooklinks.com** or scan this QR code for free additional online weblinks for further learning. These links are routinely monitored and updated to provide the most current information available.

Learn More

Archer, Joe, and Caroline Craig. *Plant, Cook, Eat! A Children's Cookbook.* Charlesbridge, 2018.

Martin, Noelle. *Super Foods for Super Kids Cookbook.* Rockridge, 2020.

Index

allergy, 27
animals, 9, 13

calcium, 12–13, 19–20,
  25, 27

fluoride, 13, 19
food group, 19, 21

immune system, 14
iodine, 7, 13, 20
iron, 13, 15, 20

major minerals, 11–12
micronutrients, 11

plant, 9, 13

sodium, 12, 14, 25
sulfur, 12, 14, 19

trace minerals, 11

zinc, 13–14, 19

About the Author

C. M. Davis is a librarian and educator. When she's not reading or writing, she enjoys bird-watching, visiting museums, and hunting for vintage treasures in thrift stores.